This book is a work of business strategies
by Gene Smith.

Small Business Marketing
Abingdon, Virginia 24210

ISBN-13: 978-1974508099

ISBN-10: 1974508099

www.firmmediadesign.com

007gene@gmail.com

Small Business Marketing

Forward

The following business strategies will work for any business.

With 42 years in the home improvement business, I've tried hundreds of business strategies, some worked, and some didn't. The ones that did were documented for future use. Although we had a large referral base, we were constantly working to find new ideas to grow our business.

Let's suppose you have been in the business for a few years and have 25 or 30 customers, (clients) but you still must prospect all the time just to keep the lights on.

What if there is a better way? <u>What if that better way got your phone to ring and people walking through your door every day, and you were getting all the business you could handle?</u> Sounds too good to be true, doesn't it? Well, there is a better way and it can work for you. It just takes a little planning to make it happen. The bottom line is you happy with the amount of money you are making?

Contents

Business Strategy #1

Stay in Touch with Your Clients!

"Profit in business comes from repeat clients, that boast about your project or service, and that bring friends with them." W. Edwards Deming

The world has changed all around us and the way we do business has changed. If you haven't been engaged in marketing for your business, then this is the time to look at the possibilities that await you.

If you have been in business for a while, then you have customers in your database or maybe even written down on a piece of paper. Wherever they are, let's dig them out and go to work on them.

Don't overlook your old clients. **They are your bread and butter!!** The most important business strategy of all is working with your existing clients. If this is true, why is it that this is the last place we look for new business when in fact, it should be the first?

Who are the people who know and trust you? You got it; they are your clients. You don't have to look elsewhere to find business; it's right under your nose. These are the people who know and trust you, so your number one strategy is working with your existing **CLIENTS.**

The reason I say clients is because a customer is someone who bought from you once while a client is an ongoing relationship.

Staying in touch with your clients is the best way I know of to get repeat business and referrals.

A great place to start is to pull out all your old client/customers and familiarize yourself with their names, what you did for them, and how much money they paid you. Then <u>pick up the phone and call them!</u>

This can be a little intimidating if they have a problem with the job you did. STOP...think about it. If they have a problem, it's a great opportunity for you to get re-acquainted with your client. Now you have an opportunity to go see them face to face and fix the problem. When you see this in the right perspective, it's no longer intimidating. Furthermore, you're glad it has been brought to your attention.

DON'T NEGLECT YOUR CLIENTS!

Fix what needs to be fixed, stay in touch with them, and you will see the referrals start rolling in, but it's more than referrals. put a plan in place, and let your clients know that you appreciate them. Make sure they always have a few of your business cards on hand. As you contact your clients each month, be sure to include a few of your business cards with your mailing.

Make sure that this is the number one thing you look at each day, write it down, or keep my book handy in your office. Do something to keep this in front of you every day. Make a daily checklist and appoint someone to carry out this task and keep you informed.

So... our #1 business strategy is: **Stay in Touch with Your Clients**. If you don't stay in touch with your clients, you won't have a need for the rest of my business strategies!

If you **are** going to stay in touch with your clients, you will need a reliable system. How many times have you had a good lead and somehow it fell through the cracks...or you just waited too long to call them and when you did, you found out that they just gave the contract to your competitor. Ouch!

The system I'm talking about is MarketSharp. The website is **www.marketsharp.com**

Here you will find a database that literally keeps up with your clients, prospects and leads. It will alert you on upcoming projects that your client or a prospective client might be considering in the future.

The system will give you new ideas on how to proceed and keep these projects in front of you. It all happens by the click of your mouse.

MarketSharp is a great way to get referrals rolling in and getting your phone to ring consistently and more importantly, keeping your clients aware of what's happening in your business.

When you are running a business, sitting in front of a computer is not what you want to be doing. You're out there making sure the job is getting done, and getting done right. Hire someone to do computer work for you. MarketSharp has online training with people standing by on the phone to answer any question and guide you step by step how to set it up.

Staying in touch with your clients will almost guarantee referrals, that is, if you have exceeded their expectations. Word-of-mouth will get out and you will reap a harvest of repeat business.

Make it easy for your clients to give you referrals!

It's important to have a referral system in place so you don't miss out.

Your clients are your number one source for leads.

Just think about all the people you can tap into just from one client. Here are a few ideas:

- Your client's relatives and friends
- Husband's father and mother
- Wife's father and mother
- Brothers and sisters
- Friends

Once you get this strategy in your mind, you will have an unlimited source of leads. One thing for sure, you won't have to go looking elsewhere for them. No more spending money on yellow page ads that don't work.

If you have done a good job for your clients, and you have stayed in touch with them, <u>they will work for you.</u>

As a matter of fact, they will go out of their way to get you leads. That's just the way it works. People like helping people they like.

If your clients are not jumping through hoops to tell others about you, then you've done something wrong.

I can't emphasize this enough, STAY IN TOUCH WITH YOUR CLIENTS.

Business Strategy #2
Referral Program

Your client is satisfied with your work and trusts you. You would think that is enough to get the referrals rolling in, but it isn't. You will have to do your part to make it happen. You surely don't want to overlook this because if you do, it will cost you plenty; so don't leave it to chance.

Make sure you make it easy for them to give you a referral. KISS (Keep it simple silly) Keep your phone number in their hands at all times by sending them a few of your business cards along with a letter, a self-addressed return envelope (include the postage), and the referral form found below.

Offer something for referrals, preferably, something you think they would like. This is your client; you should know a few things they like. Perhaps a dinner for two at a nice restaurant, topped off with tickets to the movies.

You might be thinking, "That's a lot of money", but it's not much at all when you stop to think that a lead generated by advertising cost $200 to $300 for each lead. Always think of something you can do for your client.

Here's the thing; if you have done a great job for them, they will send you referrals without you compensating them, but when you give them something or recognize them someway, the referrals will keep coming in.

So, you're going to mail them a letter, referral form, and 3 business cards. <u>You can't just do this one time; you must be persistent with it.</u> Keep your name in front of your clients. **Develop a relationship with them.**

Here's the Referral form:

Name _____

Address _____

City_____ State_____ Zip_____

Home Phone_____

Work Phone_____

Best time to call_____

Please check one:

_____ YES, please contact the above referral, as we have already talked to them, and they are expecting your call. Please feel free to use my name when you call them.

_____NO, please do not use my name when you contact the above referral. I have mentioned your name, but have not talked about you doing work for them.

Client Name _____Date_____

Put two of these forms on one page. Send a self-addressed envelope with a stamp. This works-don't short cut it.

Always keep this strategy in front of you!

Enlist your employees. Let them know what you are doing about referrals. Set some time aside to meet with them for teaching purposes and keep telling them so they understand what you expect of them. A lack of communication can be detrimental to your business.

There are other ways to get referrals. Who do you know that would be willing to pass referrals along to you? What about family members? Do they know what you are doing? You would think so, but don't assume that they do. Treat your friends the same way; let them know.

Take a few of your business cards to your realtor or maybe your favorite restaurant, only if they know you. If you don't keep something in front of people, they forget you.

If you have a real-estate friend, look him up on the internet and take his agents a few cards or mail each agent a postcard and a few business cards. I have done this and believe me, it works!!! I've had brokers ask me for cards to give to their agents. It is surprising how people are willing to help you. <u>All you have to do is ask.</u>

Join BNI (Business Networking) www.bni.com. You can attend the first meeting for free, and everyone gets your business card. Plus, you get a chance to stand up and tell about your business. There are plenty of other networking organizations that you can participate in. There is something to be said for being out-and-about.

Make a list of other things you can do to get referrals.

Business Strategy #3
Business Card

We've talked about handing out your business cards. What does your card look like? Is it professionally done? Does it have all your information listed including your website address?

Vistaprint.com is a good place to design your card. You can sign up for their Pro-Advantage and save 30 to 50% on all your orders. The pro-advantage allows you the opportunity to create an awesome card because of the extra things you can do with it.

I recommend going for a heavy paper with a gloss finish, and put something on the back of the card. All your printing materials should be the same, and Vista Print can handle that. They have a toll-free number. DO NOT HESITATE TO CALL THEM; they are more than willing to help you.

Standard size postcards are an excellent way to get your message out. They mail for $.37 ea.

Vista Print does an excellent job on door magnets for your vehicles.

You can also create a logo with Vista Print for pennies.

Here's a Powerful Business Card Strategy!

This one little business strategy will work for you even if you are "dead broke".

I've seen businesses go broke and close their doors simply because they failed to take-action. You can't just sit around hoping that business will fall out of the sky-**It Won't**! You must take action!

Anything is possible, but it takes a plan. <u>If you can imagine it, you can make it happen.</u>

Okay, here it is! Recently I developed a business card for a local business that has the potential to bring in more business that one can imagine.

The card is green and yellow with a bold print on the front side. It is easy to spot, even on a cluttered desk. The card is beautiful and tells exactly what this business does. The card is heavy paper with the business message on both sides.

The card is simple and easy to read. The fonts are bold and the words jump out at you. It's almost like they are saying "CALL ME!' Yes, that is exactly what it is saying, and that's the plan.

Now that we have this beautiful business card, we must find people to see it. We don't just want them to see it, we want them to know that our business card is something special.

Many years ago, a salesman named Sam with Hodges Supply Company from Greensboro, North Carolina, was looking at my business card on the counter. He picked it up and said, *"Gene, this little business card that cost you less than a penny a piece has the potential to bring you more business than you can imagine."*

He said, *"Every person you come across, hand them your card., It's like putting a billboard in front of their eyes. Give one to the person who pumps your gas, checks your tire pressure and cleans your windshield. (This was the old days) Give one to the waitress who serves you food. Give one to every person you meet."*

He made his point and I never forgot it a half century later.

What can this little business card do? It really is a masterpiece, and I want everyone to see it, remember it, and not throw it away. So, I intend to make a big deal of it when I hand it to them. When I offer my card, I will hold it in a manner that they realize I am proud of it. Then I say, "I just created this new business card and I want you to have one to keep." When they reach for it, I flip it over to the backside and say, "This is what I do." Then I hand them the card.

Remember, everyone gets a business card.

Be sure and pick up <u>their</u> business card for future use. Write the business owner's name on the card and try to get his/her email. <u>You will be surprised how many will give you that information.</u>

One strategy I've used over and over is go downtown and just start walking into businesses and hand out your business cards. Ask the receptionist if she is the owner as you offer her your card. Most of the time this will get a smile and then she will tell you who the owner is. Ask if he or she is in.

Okay, now you have gone to 50 businesses and left your cards, but there is a problem. You can't continue to call on more businesses because your phone is ringing off-the-hook with people who are interested in your services. You don't have time to continue knocking on doors, plus you have a pocket full of leads you picked up along the way. Just think of all the people who will be speaking to you at First Baptist Sunday morning. LOL. **Mission accomplished!**

Business Strategy #4

Business Website and Why You Need One!

Most business owners don't want to tackle a website and I don't blame them, but a business website is a must. When people see you have a professional website, they are impressed and it adds instant credibility if it is a good one.

A website is a great place to showcase all your work, job photos, and much more.

50% of small businesses don't have a website and you are going to lose business if you don't have one.

If you are searching for a business online and you see a website link, that's the one you will click on. But it's not just having a website; it's all about having a good one. A bad website is as bad as not having one at all. There is nothing more frustrating than trying to navigate through a website and half the pages don't come up, or they are very slow.

Once you get your website, it needs to be online so people can easily find it. There is an easy way to make this happen.

Take a few minutes, go to my website and look around. **www.firmmediadesign.com**. It's easy, fast, and very professional, plus it can save you a lot of money in labor cost when you're using the right one.

Our websites start at $99.00 per month with a two-year contract. You never have to pay for updates, it all comes with one package and we are always there to help you through the whole process, there is nothing for you to do except tell us how you want it done and how you want it to look. You can call us on the phone or send an email and we will take care of your needs ASAP. We do it all.

We get you online and make sure your website is fully optimized and appears on Google maps. Our goal is to get you coming up number one on google searches.

Business Strategy #5
Job Signs

One of the best marketing strategies is your job sign. Amazingly, many businesses don't use them. To me, that's the unpardonable sin.

When I was in the replacement window business, I ordered 50 at a time printed on both sides with wire stands for $5.00 each. The signs were ¼ inch perforated plastic. I carried them in my car and put them anywhere I thought was appropriate.

I always had a job sign near the road on every kitchen cabinet, carpet, and window job we did. I made a deal with the homeowner to keep the sign up for 30 days. They always did. The deal was, <u>I ASKED THEM!</u> That's it; I just simply asked. Once they sign the contract, they will agree to the sign; but if they don't like your work, forget the sign. Even if you put it up, they will take it down.

On one job, we were looking for the best place to put the job sign, and our client told us to nail it to a tree that was near the road in his front yard. It stayed there for two years. He lived on a street with very heavy traffic. That brought us plenty of business.

I see job signs along the road that are a waste of money because they have too much information on them, and most are not readable for passing traffic. Job signs should say what you do and maybe your phone number with the company name in smaller print under the phone number. That's it. People driving by can only read a word or two at most.

If you do Kitchen Cabinets, put 'Kitchen Cabinets' on the sign as big as possible with your phone number in smaller letters. Don't use any other letters or images. Yellow signs with dark blue or black letters make a good sign.

What we hope to do with a job sign is create-a-call-to-action. When people are driving by, the only thing they see is the first couple of words. If that couple of words interest them, they will take a second look, if possible.

Another idea for a job sign is a logo if you have one, and only if it is specific to what you do. For example: 'Kitchen Cabinets', 'Log Homes' or 'Carpet', etc.

You want an eye-catching color and what you do, your phone number, and company name. Keep the company name small on the bottom of the sign.

Once again, if your job sign says, 'Bill's Home Improvements' and your phone number, you probably won't get the first call. It's just too vague. It reminds me of a commercial I saw on TV. The Genie gives the guy one wish and he says, "I wish I had a million bucks." The Genie waves her wand, and one million deer appear on his front lawn.

You must be clear on what you put on the sign.

If you are <u>not</u> using job signs, you might want to really think about it. <u>A lead is a lead</u>.

Business Strategy #6
Without Exception, *MAKE YOUR CLIENT FEEL LIKE A VIP*

You've heard it said, 'The customer is always right, even if they are wrong!' *If you are ready to disengage with your client, then you may challenge them, and sometimes it's the right thing to do.*

You must find a way to deal with the fact that they are wrong. **Your need to be right can cost you a fortune.**

When you treat your client like a VIP, she will use you over and over again and never even consider another business.

She looks for the opportunity to tell someone who did her job, and if you have given her a few of your business cards, I guarantee you, she can find one in her purse. She will send you more business than you can handle.

Recently a contractor friend of mine was driving home from work at the end of a long hard day when his phone rang. It was a client who wanted to know what time he would be there today. (He had forgotten that he told her he would be there.) He looked at his watch, and even though he was 5 minutes from home and a hot meal, without hesitation he said, "I can be there in one hour." She said, "Okay." He turned his truck around and made the long drive to another city to take care of his client.

He could have made some excuse and put her off until later, but that's not his style. He genuinely cares about his clients and goes the extra mile to take care of them.

I know this client and I know how she thinks about this contractor. Even if he messes up on something, she will overlook it because she knows he will make it right.

This is rare for the industry. I have been in this business for many years and worked with a lot of contractors and it's sad to say, most don't think this way.

I've seen people who don't answer the phone the way they should. It's like you must push this button, then another, then wait and then you get cut off. For the life of me, I don't understand it. Your phone is the lifeline of your business.

Create a sense of urgency about answering your phone, and that goes for text messages and emails too.

If you can't take a call at that moment, when you get the chance, **DIAL HER NUMBER BACK!** If she has left you a message, <u>get back with her ASAP!</u> Don't make her wait, and if you don't know the answer to her question, find the answer and get back with her the same day. <u>She puts money in your bank account. LOL.</u> It's a no-brainer.

Respect your client, no matter what!

What you are trying to do with your client is to create a perfect relationship with them. We all know we can't be perfect, but if we strive to do so, we have accomplished our goal.

Business Strategy #7

Create an Unforgettable Experience for Your Client.

I'll use my own experience to illustrate a few things that we did to create an unforgettable experience for our clients. On one particular job, we were doing a kitchen make-over which tied up the use of the kitchen at lunch for a few days.

My 3 sons Brian, Greg, and Mark were doing the work. They took a lot of pride in doing the job right.

- We showed up on time to start the job the first day and every day thereafter until the job was done.
- We put up plastic so the dust would not drift through the house.
- I went by a gift shop and purchased a basket of snack goodies for our client to have something to snack on

while they were not able to use their kitchen. I made sure it was something special.

- At the end of the day, we made sure all plastic was down and dust was vacuumed so they could use part of their kitchen at night.

- When the kitchen was done, my sons presented them with a certificate of completion for them to sign and an invoice for the balance they owed. We did not leave the job until everything was satisfactory for the client.

- We followed up with a thank you letter with a few business cards.

- We also sent a letter with a testimony form to get their comments about our product and workmanship. We always got a response.

I kept a book of testimonies with me, and when I was in the home presenting our product, I pulled it out so they could read them. This was more important than anything else we did in the home.

We did more than they expected.

On one particular job, we installed solid cherry custom made cabinet doors and countertops. When the job was complete, I presented the client with a cherry canister set that was custom made to match their cabinets. They were more than impressed.

I ran into this client a year ago and she said, "My kitchen still looks like new after 20 years." She went on and on about Brian's workmanship. We created an experience they will never forget. It made us feel good about our family business.

Creating a <u>negative</u> unforgettable experience for a client is the unpardonable sin!

I hired a subcontractor to install replacement windows some years ago for a woman who was a prominent town official in our town. The sub did a good job on the windows, but while working on her house, he threw his cigarette butts on her lawn. She paid for the job, and a few days later I got a letter from her explaining how she went around her whole lawn and personally picked up all the cigarette butts. Needless to say, she was not very nice about her comments.

I confronted the subcontractor and he said, "Boy, she is really particular." He never did another job for our company.

I never got a referral from this woman and I don't blame her.

Business Strategy #8

Market Sharp Database

I did not know this website was around. I just happened upon it one day while searching the web. It has been in existence since 1998. I can't begin to tell you how big this is. When I found it, I was looking for a database that would track prospects, leads, and clients for a client of mine. I absolutely struck gold.

To start with, we will talk about the database aspect of the site. All your clients can be entered in this site and everything about the client as well. When you contact a client for any reason, the information you put in will always be available. If you have a return call date, the system will notify you when to call back.

You can keep up with a client's friends and relatives if they are a lead, or even if they are just a prospect.

Keeping up with leads is simple. Just enter them into the database and designate them as a lead or prospect, and the system will treat them as such. There is a place to enter an appointment, and the system will notify you when the appointment is due. It never fails. It works with the information you put in.

You can design postcards, flyers, letters, etc. The system will mail them out for you and keep track of the mailings and what you sent out and when it would be a good time to mail again.

You can attend webinars online within the website. You can attend home improvement & remodeling conferences. There's a world of things you can do with this system. The web address is: **www.marketsharp.com**

Business Strategy #9
My Portfolio

Today with all the technology that is available to us, our portfolio is accessible through many mediums, our website being one of them. It used to be a large notebook. This is where we keep photos of every job we do. Taking pictures of the job is a must. I made sure I had our picture taken with the client after the job was done. This is the time when the smiles are the greatest, and they are more willing to go along with you about getting their picture taken. Be sure to let them know a day ahead, or it won't happen. Women are very particular about getting their photo taken, especially if they are going to be on your website. Make sure they know your intentions for the photo.

This is important: You would think that anyone could point a camera and get a good clear photo, but that is not the way it is so find someone that can take a good photo. The iPhone works well if it is a good one. The trick to take horizontal photos for larger pixels, and make sure you are holding the camara steady when you snap the picture. You probably think I'm going overboard with this, but I'm not. You only get one chance at it, so do it right. When you click on that photo in your client page of your website and the picture pops up enlarged, you just want it right and impressive.

If your website is optimized properly, you can show your client jobs right on your iPhone or tablet. A good example of this is **www.nealragan.com**. Take a look at the site, especially the client pages.

All of this takes time, but it's worth it many times over. It is an excellent closing tool.

After showing off your website and clients pages and when you are ready to leave, be sure to leave your hard copy of your portfolio and a couple extra business cards.

First impressions make all the difference

A few days ago, a guy was working on the lawn next door, so I went over and asked him to give me a price on a small job, he did and then done the job. I liked his work and thought I would get him to do more, but he didn't leave me a business card, much less a portfolio. He didn't have a sign on his truck and I don't remember his name.

People who are making a lot of money in this business are doing all these things mentioned in my book. So how do I remember all these strategies every day? The answer is to read my book every day and keep it handy. Act on these strategies.

Business Strategy #10
Testimonials

I started a replacement window business in 1989 and by 2000, we had 325 clients. Over a period of time, we had accumulated many letters of testimonials. I put the original copies in a notebook, along with names and addresses of every client we had and carried it with me on every appointment.

As the prospect started looking through it, they would begin talking about the ones they knew. I was always amazed how much time they spent with it. I spent as much time as possible just letting them look, without saying a word. There is power in testimonial letters and client names.

I highly recommend a notebook as well as having them on your website.

When I started collecting these letters, I was amazed at all the nice things people had to say about our company, our three sons (who installed the windows and kitchens), and my wife Nancy, who ran the office. We had a very successful window and kitchen business.

Getting our hands on these letters was not easy. We mailed out our testimonial form, and the people responded by writing back with their letters or simply filling out the form and returning it.

When a job was complete, we mailed a letter and form the next day. We always sent a self-addressed, stamped envelope along with the letter. We didn't get all of them, but we got our share.

Business Strategy #11
Becoming a Business Owner and Contractor

If you want to become a business owner, I suggest you go to this website **www.sba.gov** and make an appointment to talk with someone representing your area.

I've learned a few things over the past 42 years, but I do not pretend to know the laws on businesses in Virginia or any other state. There are a few things I know and will share according to my own experiences.

I do know that if you plan to be a contractor business owner in Virginia, you will need to have a state license as well as town/county, etc. and proper insurances. Liability and workman's compensation is required.

If you plan to do business in another state, you will need all the license that they require, as well as town license.

There are contractors and businesses on every corner that are operating a business without any kind of license at all-**THAT'S A HUGE MISTAKE!** To say the least. If a state or local official confronts you, it will cost you a lot in fines and you may even lose what you have, or worse yet, end up in jail.

Some homeowners encourage workers by not checking out a person's credentials to see if they have a license and insurance, simply because of greed. They take a big chance just to save money. The homeowner is taking a huge risk by working someone who does not have a license.

Several years ago, I read about someone who contracted with a contractor to redo their driveway. They made a deal with him without knowing if he was licensed and even paid him half the money down. He brought his front-end loader and dump truck, then removed all the existing asphalt and hauled it to the landfill.

He was leveling out the dirt when a state official walked up and asked for his license. Of course, he did not have a license of any kind. The sheriff then showed up and arrested him. All of his equipment was impounded. Later on, they sold his equipment to pay the fines. Suddenly the man found himself out of business and still in big trouble.

During this time, the homeowner had to hire another contractor to finish their driveway. They lost all of the down payment they paid to the first man, so the job cost almost double. This could have cost them a lot more; what if the contractor had damaged their house in some way, or hurt someone at the homeowner's property? He had no insurance, workman's comp or anything.

The homeowner would be responsible for fixing their house, plus, if someone got hurt, they could be sued for medical bills, workman's comp, liability, and the list just keeps getting bigger. Since the contractor had none of these things, the homeowner would become liable.

The contractor is liable for putting the homeowner in such a situation, so the homeowner sues the contractor. He's already lost everything, so the homeowner gets nothing This stays with the contractor for years to come. If he ever crawls out of the hole, he is still liable to pay the fines and damages. Something like this can wipe you out for a lifetime. It's just not worth the risk, and yet it goes on every day.

<u>Get the license and insurance required or just work for someone else.</u> Just a suggestion.

A contractor is required to carry workman's comp insurance in most states, even if he is the only one working.

The Contract

The days of doing work for people by a handshake is history. In the state of Virginia, a contractor is required to have a written contract stating what he is going to do, and you are required by federal law to present the homeowner with their right to cancel the job in three days from the date of the contract.

To get such a contract drafted up, you will need a lawyer.

Your contract has to protect you as well as the homeowner and the three-day cancellation clause has to be on your contract in bold lettering. Also, there might be another form required.

Here's what can happen if you do not have the three-day cancellation on your contract:

I wrote a contract for 21 replacement windows (which were all custom made and wood grain). The contract was signed by the home owner and I ordered the windows. A couple of weeks later the homeowner's two daughters walked into my office and informed me that they wanted to cancel their father's order for the windows. I told them that they couldn't cancel because I had already ordered them and they were all custom made to fit his window openings.

They informed me that they had just come from their attorney's office, and he informed them that because there was not a three-day cancellation clause in the contract, they could cancel at any time.

When they left my office, I threw away all my contracts and had new ones printed with the three-day clause.

If there had been no contract, it would have been the same. It's highly possible to do a big job for someone and not even get paid for it at all, and it would be perfectly legal for the homeowner to do so.

Business Strategy #12
Direct Mail

The USPS, Vista Print and Market have a business mailing program that is the best I've seen. You can mail your flyer, postcard etc. to about any target you choose.

Today I chose a section of town that has some of the nicer homes in our city. I did a search on USPS website and came up with 593 homes that the post office will deliver my direct mail advertising piece for $108.52. That's 18 cents each. If you only get a 1% return, that's 6 leads. If you close four of those, that's pretty good money.

What if you got a 10% return on your mailing? That's 59 leads. If you only closed 12, that's pretty good. If you made a profit of $1,500.00 on each one, then that's $18,000.00 in the bank. Your profit margin could go up to $50,000.00, or more.

Here's a link that will take you to their website: **www.usps.com** or call them.

Business Strategy #13

Letters & How to Get Them Opened

If you are going to mail a letter to someone about a special promotion you have going on, then here's a way to make sure they get opened.

When I go to my mailbox, I come back by the trash can to sort through it. I can tell by looking at the envelope if it's an advertisement or not, I trash more mail than I open.

Here's a little trick that will guarantee the person who get your letter will open it. Here's how; write their name and address with a blue ball point pen and write your return address with only the street, city, state, and zip at the top left. Be sure the envelope is a security type. Now your piece of mail looks like it's from a friend or maybe a family member. That's it, they will open it.

Occasionally, I get mail that the sender has tried to make it look this way, but there is only one way, **the pen must touch the paper**. People are smart and can tell instantly if it's printed or handwritten. I don't open the printed ones.

If you, do it right, I guarantee you, it will be opened!

If you mail to the same person again, have a different person address the envelope. The return address should be different as well. People are smart; they remember your handwriting.

Here's another little trick that works great as well. While you are doing a job in a neighborhood, mail a letter with your letter head and an envelope with your business name printed on it. Hopefully, you have a very attractive envelope to do this.

Here's how to locate the names of the people who live near the job. Login to your **MarketSharp** website and do a search for people who live near the job you are doing and print it out. **MarketSharp** will also design and mail postcards for you. You can search for the homeowner's address, city, state, and zip. The search will show if they are the homeowners. In most cases, your letter will be opened because they have seen your vehicles in the neighborhood.

Business Strategy #14

Branding Your Business

What is branding? It's hard to answer this in just a word or two. A logo is a kind of brand, but it's much more than that. It's what you're telling your clients when you do what you say you will do. Branding is something that occurs when you do the right thing or bad thing. When you build trust and integrity, branding follows. It's your business reputation. Branding is simple but complex.

How people see you is your brand. Your brand might project you as a trustworthy person, or a deadbeat who never does what he says he will do. It follows you around and brands you. It never lies. You are what you are.

You are branded in your everyday life; people know you for how you've lived your life and performed.

When people see your logo, what do they see? The image that comes into their minds is your brand. When you see those golden arches, the first thing you think of is a hamburger, but not just any hamburger;

it's a Big Mac, and it's good. McDonald's brand is good food, great service, and a clean facility.

When you see Lowes's logo, you immediately see all the building products. They have been years creating their brand.

I've built a few houses and one thing that is more important than anything else is the foundation. It's the starting point for everything else to fit on. Your business logo and brand is that foundation.

When people see your logo, do they think of trust and integrity, or he doesn't do what he says he will do? Your complete brand is connected to your logo. It's like your DNA; everything in it is yours, but in this case, you've created it by your actions.

Your website communicates your brand. Every small detail on your website is describing your brand. The client page with all the photos is describing your brand. The visible logo on your site should say worthy, trust, and integrity.

When people see your logo, they should think of the best workmanship and quality products. For this reason, your price is justified. They know you will deliver.

When you see Pepsi Cola, you know it will be good and you don't mind paying a little more than the other sodas. Their brand says it all.

As a business owner, what is your mission? What you intend your business to be will become part of your brand. Have you written out your mission? It might be something you seriously want to think about.

What are the benefits of your products and services? This is something that needs to be documented.

Do you know what your clients think of you and your company? This cannot be left to chance; this is something we all have to know. If you have been in business for a while, you should already have a feel for this. You are the only person who can know.

Create a unique logo. It can't just be good; it must be great!

Be consistent with all your printing documents. Keep everything uniform. Keep your logo in front of people and make it visible.

Business Strategy #15

Lifetime Value of a Client

I was hired by a company to connect with all their clients. They had been in business for 25 years and had 3500 clients. I set up an office and started calling these clients and they were asking me, "Who did you say this was?" I'd repeat the name and they had no recollection of this company ever doing anything for them. I went to the owner of the business and asked how often he called these clients since he had done their work? He said, "We never called them after the job was done."

I realized very fast that most of these folks were customers, not clients.

The outcome to this was that they ended up with about 500 clients and the rest did not know who they were. All of these 3500 could have been clients if the company had stayed in touch with them. It is no telling how many millions of dollars they lost.

What if they had stayed in touch with all these people? The lifetime value is to keep a client as long as you are in business. If a client is happy with your work, they will tell others about you and pass referrals on to you. I have a friend whose average job is $75,000.00. If he made a 30% profit, that's $22,500.00. The referrals a client gives you over a lifetime could amount to millions.

Business Strategy #16

The Importance of a Unique Selling Proposition

What is a USP (Unique Selling Proposition?)

It is a statement that sets you apart from your competitors. It is sometimes confused with a tagline which is used to grab attention. A USP is a statement about your company.

Why should someone choose you over your competitor? What can you offer that your competitors can't? Without A USP, you appear just like all the other guys. It's not an easy task to come up with, but very essential for your company. Below are a few ideas:

M&M's: "Melts in your mouth, not in your hand."

FedEx: "When your package absolutely, positively has to get there overnight."

Saddleback Leather: "They'll fight over it when you're dead."

Mast Brothers Chocolate: "We're from the 18th century, back when craftspeople were revered and took pride in working with their hands."

Once you come up with your personal USP, you will want it to appear with your company name. It becomes part of your name.

Don't rush into picking your USP; take your time and get it right.

To get a better understanding of a USP, I suggest that you check out Brian Tracy's definition on YouTube.

Business Strategy #17

12 Questions to Ask a Business Owner or Contractor Before You place the order.

1. **Are you licensed?** If he can't confirm this question, then there is nowhere to go with this contractor. Save yourself a lot of time; **don't hire him** because he is breaking the law. If he says yes, that is well and good; but if he's legit, he won't mind giving you a copy of his 'State Contractor's License' (if one is required in your state) and town license as well.

   Almost every town requires a business or contractor to purchase a license to do business in that town, and most towns require a contractor to present proof that he has an up to date state contractor's license before he gets a town license.

   The business or contractor should have a copy of his 'State Contractors License' and a copy of his 'town license' in his portfolio that he has given to you. Be sure to check the dates to make sure both licenses are up to date, and if it's not clear, then you will have to contact the State board of license. (In Virginia, that is Richmond)

This is so important. It's not good enough just to confirm that he has all the license to do business, you must know what type of state license he has. In Virginia, there is an 'A', 'B' and 'C'. If he is operating with a 'C', it might not be adequate to cover the amount of your contract, and a host of other things as well. Most contractors will have a 'B' type, 'A' is best.

If you live in a townhouse, gated community, or a golf community, etc. only a licensed contractor or building contractor with the special designation can do business in these communities.

By doing a little upfront work you can save yourself a lot of heartache and money. DO NOT HIRE AN UNLICENSED BUSINESS OR CONTRACTOR!!!

2. **Do you carry liability insurance?** Property owner's liability insurance covers lawsuits arising from property damage or injury to someone visiting your property, like a contractor, his employees, sub-contractors, delivery personnel, etc.

   Here is an example: What if someone came on your property and stepped on a nail sticking up through a board the contractor carelessly left lying on the ground and the person ended up in the ER a few days later with a huge hospital bill. Who is responsible for the bill? If they sue you, you are responsible for the bill. If the contractor has liability insurance, then his insurance company is responsible. If the contractor doesn't have liability insurance, and you don't have liability, then you, the homeowner will have to pay it out of your pocket.

3. **Do you carry Worker's Compensation Insurance?** Worker's compensation insurance is a form of insurance that provides wage replacement and medical benefits to an employee who is injured in the line of duty.

   If a contractor or his employees get hurt while working at your home, then his workmen's comp will pay wage replacement and medical bills. If he <u>does not </u>have workmen's comp, then you or your insurance may be liable.

In some states, a one-man company may not be legally required to carry workmen's comp, but if he doesn't have it, who will be obligated to pay a claim? Here again, the home may be liable.

You cannot take a chance on this. You must know if the business or contractor carries Workmen's Compensation Insurance.

There is a way a business or contractor can have workmen's comp without carrying the traditional type insurance. One that I know of is Paychecks. They will cover a business and his employees as they work per job. Here again, you will have to check it out. If he uses subcontractors on your job, then how would they be covered?

These are the questions that you just have to know. One claim could cause you to have to sell your house to pay a lawsuit. I know it's kind of scary, but it is a reality. www.paychex.com

4. **Will you provide references?** Again, the business or contractor's portfolio should contain some of his references in it. If it doesn't, be sure to ask for them. Once you have them, call them up and ask about the job the contractor did for them and if they are satisfied with his work.

If you get three or four who are satisfied, then that is probably a good indication that he is okay. If someone invites you to come out and look at their work, <u>I would surely do it.</u>

5. **Will you pull all building permits?** Many businesses and contractors don't like to do it because it takes a lot of time. Also, if a business or contractor does not have a license, he will not attempt it. However, it is very important that the contractor takes care of it. This way, he is aware of all the building codes.

The business or contractor should have the cost of permits figured in the contract to take care of paying for them.

The business/owner or contractor, as well as the homeowner, should be directly working with the building inspector to make sure everything is up to code.

6. **Do you give a written guarantee on your work?** Most companies will give a year guarantee. Some may give 2 or 3 years. Why not give a lifetime?

7. **What does the contract cover?** If it's not in the contract, don't assume it will get done. Maybe something was verbally mentioned, but not in

the contract. Be sure that everything is in the contract that is supposed to be done.

The contract should have the start and finish date.

The contract should spell out how the business or contractor intends to keep the job neat and clean. Will they clean up every day? Will the contractor keep the home free of dust and debris? You are a client now, and your needs matter.

By law, the contract must have the three-day cancellation clause in bold fonts.

Most of us can't write out a contract, so here is a link that will tell you everything you need to know. Keep in mind that contracts are not free; you will have to spend a little money to have one drafted to fit your unique situation of doing business, but this is something that has to be correct. **www.rocketlawyer.com**

8. **Who is your crew?** If you are using subcontractors, it is important that the homeowner knows who they are and if they have the proper license and insurance to conduct business as a contractor.

The homeowner needs to know specifically who is going to be in their home and who is going to be in charge when the contractor is away from the job?

The homeowner needs to know as much as possible who is going to be in and out of their home, with no exceptions!

9. **How do you expect payment?** This is something that most definitely will be in the contract, but it needs to be talked about extensively so there are no misunderstandings. Everything hinges on the money!

10.**Will there be any hazardous materials on the job and if so, how will they be handled?** One thing comes to my mind is lead. If a house was painted before 1978, it most likely has lead in the paint. Proper removal must be followed to the letter.

11.**What time will you show up on the job from day to day?** The contractor should provide the homeowner a written schedule when they will be on the job and what time they will leave the job each day. In other words, the contractor should communicate all schedules. And the contractor should be clear on how that communication will be done, such as a phone call, texting or email.

12. What will be done to keep my home safe?

Under no circumstances should a stranger wonder in on the job and have access to the homeowner's home.

A business or contractor should never leave a job with power equipment still plugged into a receptacle. The job location should be free of danger at all times.

About the Author

In 1957 my father started a storm window and door business with no money. I doubt if he foresaw what the business would become. I'm sure I didn't, but the timing was right and that made a big difference.

In 1957, I was 14 years old and still in school. I worked in his business in the afternoon after school for $0.50 an hour and was glad I had a job. Most guys my age did not have a job.

The first job we did, we didn't even have an office. My father was working from his home. We lived in a small 3-bedroom house with no basement. There was no place to store windows. My father had burned all the bridges behind him when he decided to get into the business, so it was sink or swim. I assure you it was a scary time for him with a wife and 4 kids to feed.

My father was a plumber and we had moved from Marion, Virginia, to Orlando, Florida looking for a better life. There was more work and that helped a little. We were living like everyone else-from pay check to pay check. After a year we moved to Cocoa, Florida, about 40 miles away. That saved on travel time. After living there for a year, a friend of my father came to see him. It must have been important because he drove all the way from Virginia to Florida.

The friend (Telsie Blevins) realized an opportunity existed back in Virginia. In 1957 no one had storm windows or storm doors. It was something new and he felt that he and my father could do well with it. He convinced my father to come back to Virginia and start a window company. At that time, there was another company in Marion called Fox Window and Awning Company owned and operated by Mr. Lee Fox. He was definitely doing well with the window business.

My father took Telsie at his word and decided to give it a try, so we moved back to Virginia.

Somehow my father managed to buy a 1937 Chevrolet truck to use to haul windows. Our first job was 10 storm windows and 2 storm doors. The day we installed the windows, it was pouring the snow and the wind was blowing so hard you could barely see the windows. We didn't have a choice; we had to get this job done to buy groceries and pay for the windows.

My father and Telsie Blevins knocked on doors, rain or shine. They were a good team. Telsie was a powerful, enthusiastic person. I talked to him on the phone a few days ago. He's the only one still alive from the old days.

He and my father were heroes of the day!

Notes

Notes

Notes

Notes

Notes